Home Organization: Your Life

or monetary loss due to the information herein, either directly or indirectly.

Table of content

Chapter 1: Getting Started..................4

1A: Assessing Your Current Situation.......6

1B: Setting Goals.................8

Chapter 2: Decluttering Process...............10

2A: Mindful Decluttering...............12

2B: Room-by-Room Decluttering..............14

Chapter 3: Organization Strategies...............16

3A: Storage Solutions............... 18

3B: Time-Management Techniques...............20

Chapter 4: Life Changes...............22

4A: Letting Go of Stuff...............24

4B: Adopting New Habits...............26

Chapter 5: Maintaining Organization...............28

5A: Regular Cleaning...............30

5B: Staying on Track............... 32

Chapter 6: Finishing Up............... 34

6A: Celebrating Success............... 36

6B: Preparing for the Future............... 38

Chapter 1: Getting Started

It can be overwhelming to look around and realize that your living space is cluttered and disorganized. But it's important to remember that all it takes is a little bit of effort and dedication to get your home organized and keep it that way. This chapter will provide you with the basics to get started on your journey to a tidier and more organized home.

The first step is to assess the situation. Take a look around your home and determine which areas need the most help. Do you have a lot of clothes and other items that no longer serve a purpose or that you don't use? Is there a lot of stuff lying around that you don't know what to do with? Make a list of all of the areas that need attention so that you can focus your efforts.

Once you have a list of areas that need work, it's time to start decluttering. This means getting rid of items that you no longer need or use. Start by sorting through all of your belongings. Sort them into piles of items that you want to keep, items that you want to donate or give away, and items that you want to throw away. If it's been a while since you've gone through your belongings, you may be surprised at how much you can get rid of.

Once you've decluttered your belongings, it's time to start organizing. Start by creating a plan for each area of your home. Think about what you use the most and how you can make it easier to access those items. For instance, if you have a lot of clothes, consider setting up a closet system to keep them organized.

Next, set up a filing system for important documents, such as bills and bank statements. This will make it easier to find them when you need them without having to dig through piles of paper.

Finally, set up a system for everyday items, such as mail, keys, and remotes. This will help to keep these items from getting misplaced and will make it easier to find them when you need them.

Getting your home organized and decluttered can be a daunting task, but it doesn't have to be overwhelming. With some effort and dedication, you can have a clutter-free home that is easy to keep clean and organized. All it takes is a plan and some hard work.

1A: Assessing Your Current Situation

Before beginning the journey to a clutter-free life, it is important to assess your current situation. Take a look around and determine the areas of your home that are overflowing with possessions. Do you have a closet that is too full of clothes, or a kitchen countertop that is consistently covered with items? Maybe your pantry is bursting at the seams with non-perishable food, or your garage is so packed that you can't fit a car in it. Make a list of the areas that need to be organized and prioritize them.

Next, consider the types of possessions that are causing the clutter. Are you an avid collector of items, such as books, CDs, or DVDs? Is your desk covered with paperwork that needs to be sorted? Do you have a storage area that is full of seasonal decorations? Make a list of the items that need to be organized and prioritize them as well.

Now that you have identified the areas and items that need to be organized, it is time to assess your lifestyle and determine how the clutter affects you. Do you feel overwhelmed by the amount of clutter in your home? Is it difficult to find items when you need them? Do you often feel embarrassed by the condition of your home when guests come over? Consider how the clutter is impacting your life and make note of it.

Finally, take a look at your current organizational habits. Do you have any systems in place to help you stay organized? Do you have any routines that you follow to keep the clutter at bay? Make a list of the current organizational habits that you have in place, and consider which ones could use some improvement.

By assessing your current situation, you can determine the areas of your home that need to be organized and the types of possessions that are causing the clutter. You can also consider how the clutter is impacting your life and identify any organizational habits that you may need to improve. With this information, you can begin your journey to a clutter-free life.

1B: Setting Goals

Having a clear set of goals is essential for achieving success and organization in any endeavor. Goals provide focus and direction, and they help motivate you to take action and stay on track. When it comes to home organization, setting goals is especially important.

When setting goals, it is important to keep in mind the SMART framework. Goals should be Specific, Measurable, Attainable, Relevant, and Time-Bound. Specific goals are ones that are clearly stated and easy to understand. Measurable goals are ones that have a concrete way to measure progress. Attainable goals are ones that are realistic and achievable. Relevant goals are those that are meaningful to you and align with your overall objectives. Time-bound goals are those that have a set timeline for completion.

When setting goals for home organization, it is important to focus on one area at a time. For example, you may choose to focus on organizing your bedroom first, or on decluttering your kitchen. Once you have identified the area you want to focus on, you can break down your goals into small, manageable tasks. This will make the process of achieving your goal more manageable and easier to track.

Another important factor to consider when setting home organization goals is to be realistic. While it is important to challenge yourself and set ambitious goals, it is also important to set goals that are achievable. Setting goals that are too lofty or unrealistic may lead to frustration and discouragement.

Finally, it is important to identify a timeline for achieving each goal. This will help keep you on task and motivated to finish. It is also important to remember to be flexible and adjust your timeline as needed.

By following the SMART framework and setting realistic goals, you will be well on your way to achieving success in home organization. Keeping your goals in mind and staying focused will help ensure that you make progress and reach your goals.

Chapter 2: Decluttering Process

Decluttering can be an overwhelming process, but it doesn't have to be. With the right plan and the right mindset, anyone can get their home organized.

The first step is to assess the space. Take a look around and determine what items should stay and what should go. Make sure to think through each item and how it is used. If it has not been used in awhile, it might be time to part ways.

Next, create a sorting system. This will help to keep things organized and make the process easier. Choose three categories: keep, donate, and discard. Place all items into one of these categories. This is also a great time to involve family members and get their input on what should stay.

Once the sorting is complete, it is time to start the actual decluttering process. Start with the items that will be discarded. These items should be thrown away or recycled. Items that can be donated should be placed in the designated area for donation. The remaining items should be put back in their appropriate places.

Now that the main decluttering process is complete, it is important to maintain the space. Set up a plan for how often the space will be decluttered. This will help to keep the space organized and free of clutter. Make sure to check the space regularly and get rid of anything that is no longer needed.

Decluttering can be a daunting process, but with the right plan and attitude, it can be a rewarding experience. Taking the time to assess, sort, and declutter will help to create a more organized and stress-free home. With the right set of tools and a little bit of effort, anyone can transform their home into a clutter-free paradise.

2A: Mindful Decluttering

Decluttering your home can be an overwhelming process, but it doesn't have to be. Mindful decluttering is a way to approach the task of organizing your home in a way that is both efficient and meaningful. By taking a mindful approach to decluttering, you can make the process manageable and enjoyable, rather than overwhelming.

The key to mindful decluttering is to be mindful of your intentions and needs. Before you begin the process, take some time to think about what you want to accomplish and why. Think about what items you need to keep, what items you can discard, and what items you can donate. Focus on the present and think about how you can create a space that meets your current needs.

Once you have a clear intention for the decluttering process, you can begin to sort through your possessions. As you go through each item, take some time to reflect on the purpose it serves in your life. Ask yourself whether it is still serving that purpose. If it is not, consider whether you can let it go.

As you sort through your possessions, it is important to be mindful of your relationship with them. Be mindful of the stories and memories associated with each item and be honest with yourself about whether or not they still serve a purpose in your life. Consider the emotions that come up when you think about the item. If it stirs up negative feelings, it may be time to let it go.

Mindful decluttering is about more than just getting rid of things you don't need. It is also about letting go of the emotional attachments you have to those items. By allowing yourself to let go of items that no longer serve a purpose in your life, you can create a space that is organized and meaningful.

When you have finished decluttering, take some time to appreciate the space you have created. Recognize the work you have done to create this organized space, and give yourself permission to enjoy it. This will make the process of maintaining your organized space more enjoyable and manageable.

By taking a mindful approach to decluttering, you can make the process of organizing your home less overwhelming and more meaningful. Take your time and be mindful of your intentions and needs, and you will be able to create a space that reflects your values and serves your current needs.

2B: Room-by-Room Decluttering

Decluttering is an essential part of organizing your home. It can be a daunting task, but breaking it down into smaller, manageable tasks can make the process more manageable. This will outline a room-by-room approach to decluttering your home.

Start by tackling one room at a time. Begin by gathering all items that do not belong in that room and put them in designated areas according to their destination. For example, any items that are meant for the kitchen should be placed in the kitchen area.

Once you have removed items that do not belong in the room, start organizing the remaining items. Begin by sorting items into categories, such as clothes, books, toys, etc. Then, within each category, sort items by type, size, and color. This will help you determine what items can be kept and what should be discarded.

Once you have sorted your items, it's time to start decluttering. Begin by removing items that are no longer useful or of any value. For example, clothing that no longer fits, books that you have already read, and toys that are no longer played with. Any items that you decide to keep should be organized into designated areas or containers.

After you have decluttered your room, it's time to clean. Dust shelves, vacuum carpets, and wipe down surfaces. This will make the room look and feel more organized.

When you have finished decluttering and cleaning the room, it's time to review your work. Check for any items you may have missed, and make sure that all items are in their designated areas or containers.

Decluttering your home room-by-room is a great way to get organized and stay organized. Taking the time to sort, declutter, and clean each room can make a big difference in the look and feel of your home. With a little effort, you can make your home more organized and clutter-free.

Chapter 3: Organization Strategies

Organization is key to maintaining a clutter-free home. Without a plan, it can be difficult to stay on top of the daily tasks needed to keep a home clean and orderly. Fortunately, there are strategies that can help anyone keep their home organized and free of clutter.

The first step in any organizational strategy is to create a designated space for all items. Even if the home is small, it is important to have a place for everything. This includes a central area for all paperwork and mail, as well as separate areas for shoes, coats, and other items. Designate a place for each item and make sure it is kept in its designated area.

The next step is to create a filing system. This system should be tailored to the individual's needs. A system can be as simple as filing all paperwork in a folder or as complex as creating a filing cabinet with multiple drawers. It is important to find a filing system that works for the individual and to make sure all paperwork is kept up to date.

Once a filing system is established, it is important to create a schedule. Scheduling daily, weekly, and monthly tasks helps keep track of what needs to be done and helps ensure that nothing is forgotten. Scheduling tasks can also help prevent clutter from piling up.

Creating a checklist is another way to stay organized. Checklists can be used to keep track of items that need to be purchased, tasks that need to be done, and items that need to be put away. Having a checklist makes it easier to keep track of what needs to be done and helps ensure that nothing is forgotten.

Organizing the home doesn't have to be a daunting task. By creating a designated space for each item, establishing a filing system, scheduling tasks, and creating checklists, anyone can keep their home organized and clutter-free. With a few simple strategies, anyone can declutter their life and create a home environment that is both organized and relaxing.

3A: Storage Solutions

Organizing your home can seem overwhelming and intimidating, but with the right storage solutions, it doesn't have to be. Finding ways to store your items in a neat and efficient way can help to make your home look and feel more organized and put together.

The first step to finding the right storage solutions for your home is to take inventory of what you have and where it should go. This will help you to better understand what types of storage you need and what size and shape will be best for your space.

Once you have a better idea of what you need, it's time to find the right storage solutions. Shelves can be a great way to display items and keep them organized. Floating shelves are a great option for smaller spaces since they don't take up much room. You can also find wall-mounted shelves or storage cubes that can be arranged in different ways to create a custom storage solution.

For items that you don't want to display, consider finding storage bins or baskets to store them. Plastic bins are great for items that you can't hang or shelves, such as out of season clothing or bedding. Wicker baskets can be used to store items such as magazines and books, or to keep small items organized.

If you have items that you need to keep but don't use very often, consider investing in some storage containers. Containers with lids are great for items such as seasonal decorations or photos and keepsakes. You can also use containers to store items in the garage or shed.

Finally, if you don't have much room for storage, consider using vertical storage solutions. Wall-mounted coat racks or hooks can be used to hang jackets, hats, and bags. Over-the-door shoe organizers can be used to store shoes and other items.

By finding the right storage solutions, you can make your home more organized and make it easier to find what you need when you need it. With the right storage solutions, your home can become a much cleaner and more organized place to live.

3B: Time-Management Techniques

Time-management techniques are essential to staying organized and productive. There are many approaches that can be taken to ensure time is used efficiently and effectively.

The first step to effective time-management is to identify what tasks are most important and need to be prioritized. This can be done by creating a to-do list and placing tasks in order of importance. Once the list is created, it is important to set aside time each day to focus on each task.

Another technique to use is to break down tasks into smaller, achievable goals. This will help to stay motivated and increase productivity. Additionally, it is important to set deadlines for each task. Deadlines should be realistic and give enough time to complete the task.

Delegating tasks is another method for effective time-management. This can be done by enlisting help from family or friends. This will help reduce the amount of time needed to accomplish tasks and allow more time for other activities.

Having a daily schedule is also important to stay organized and productive. Scheduling time for specific tasks and activities will help to keep track of what needs to be done and when. Additionally, leaving some time for relaxation is key to avoiding burnout.

Finally, it is important to eliminate distractions. Social media, phone calls, and emails can be time-consuming and take away from important tasks. Turning off notifications and setting time limits for activities can help to stay on track and stay organized.

By implementing these time-management techniques, it is possible to stay organized and productive. By prioritizing tasks, breaking them into achievable goals, delegating tasks, creating a daily schedule, and eliminating distractions, it is possible to declutter one's life and stay organized.

Chapter 4: Life Changes

The fourth chapter of this book is about life changes. It is undeniable that life includes changes, big and small. Life changes can come in many forms and can occur at any given time. It is important to stay organized and to plan ahead for any upcoming changes in order to make the transition smoother.

The first step in preparing for life changes is to assess the situation. Look at the current circumstances and determine what needs to be done. It is important to make a list of any tasks that need to be completed in order to ensure a successful transition. This could include making a budget, researching the new area or job, or packing up belongings.

It is also important to take the time to declutter and downsize before a life change. This includes sorting through belongings and getting rid of any items that are no longer needed. This could be done by donating or selling items to make the transition easier. It is also important to consider what items are essential and will be needed in the new situation.

The next step is to create a plan for the transition. This includes making a timeline of when tasks need to be completed, setting deadlines, and breaking down the process into smaller steps. It is important to stay organized and to keep track of any progress that has been made. It is also important to stay focused on the goal and to stay motivated.

It is also important to make sure to take care of oneself during the transition. This includes making time for self-care, getting enough sleep, exercising, and eating healthy. It is also important to reach out for help and support when needed, such as talking to family and friends, or seeking professional help.

Finally, it is important to be flexible and to be prepared for any changes that may occur during the process. Life changes can be unpredictable and it is important to be ready for any surprises. It is also important to be patient and to try to stay positive during the transition.

Life changes can be difficult, but it is important to be prepared and to stay organized. Taking the time to plan ahead and to declutter can help make the transition smoother. It is also important to take care of oneself during the process and to be flexible with any unexpected changes.

4A: Letting Go of Stuff

Letting go of stuff can be a challenging process for many people. It can be difficult to part with items that have sentimental value, or those that were expensive and have been used for a long time. Although it is hard to do, it is sometimes necessary to make room for new items and to simplify your life.

The first step to letting go of stuff is to be honest with yourself. Make a list of the items you are willing to part with and those that you are not. This will help you to be clear about what you want to keep and what you are willing to let go of.

The next step is to evaluate the items you want to keep. Ask yourself if the item still has a purpose in your life or if it is taking up valuable space. If the item is still useful, consider whether it can be stored in a more compact way or if it can be donated.

The third step is to take action. If you have decided to part with an item, you should dispose of it responsibly. If the item is still in good condition, you can donate it or sell it. If it is damaged, you should recycle it or dispose of it in an environmentally friendly way.

Finally, the fourth step is to let go of the emotional attachment to the items. Remind yourself that the items are just things and that you can live without them.

Letting go of stuff is an important part of decluttering and simplifying your life.

Letting go of stuff can be a difficult process, but it is an important step in organizing your home. By following these four steps, you can make it easier to part with items that you no longer need and make room for new items. By taking the time to assess your belongings and let go of items that are no longer useful, you can create a more organized and simpler home.

4B: Adopting New Habits

There is no denying that it can be a challenge to break bad habits and form new ones. It may feel like a daunting task, but with the right guidance and dedication, it is possible to adopt new habits that will help you with your home organization goals.

The first step in changing habits is to identify which ones need to be changed. Having a clear understanding of the habit or habits you want to change will make the process easier. Once you know what habits you need to change, you can develop a plan to make the change.

Creating a plan of action is one of the most important steps in forming a new habit. Having an organized plan of attack will make it much easier to stay on track. Start by setting a timeline for yourself. Don't set goals that are too ambitious, as this can lead to frustration and failure. Instead, set small achievable goals that will help you to build momentum.

In order to ensure that you stick to your plan, it is important that you create a system of accountability. Ask a family member or a friend to check in with you on a regular basis to make sure that you are on track. This will help to remind you of your goals and will help to keep you motivated.

Another way to stay on track is to track your progress. Noting each step you take towards your goal will help you to stay on track and will help you to see how far you have come. It is also important to reward yourself for the successes you have along the way.

Finally, don't forget to be patient. Forming new habits takes time and dedication. Don't give up if you stumble along the way. Take each day one step at a time and don't be afraid to ask for help if you need it. With the right guidance and dedication, you can create habits that will help you with your home organization goals.

Chapter 5: Maintaining Organization

Maintaining a well-organized home is not a one-time task. It requires effort and dedication, and it is important to stay on top of it. Developing good habits and routines is key to maintaining a clutter-free home.

To begin, start by creating an organizational system. Create categories that make sense for the items in your home. For example, if you have a lot of books, create a bookshelf and sort the books alphabetically or by genre. This will make it easier to locate items when needed.

When organizing your home, it is also important to create designated areas for items. Have a spot for everything and make sure that items are returned to their designated areas once they are used. This will help keep clutter at bay and make it easier to find items when needed.

In addition to having designated areas for items, it is also important to be consistent with tidying up. Make it a daily habit to put away items that are out of place and wipe down surfaces. This will help keep your home looking clean and organized.

It is also important to stay on top of larger maintenance tasks, such as deep cleaning and organizing. Schedule cleaning days throughout the year to make sure you don't fall behind on these tasks. This will help keep your home in order and make it easier to stay organized.

Finally, it is important to routinely declutter your home. Go through items that you no longer need or use and donate or recycle them. This will help keep items from piling up and make it easier to find what you need.

These are just a few tips to help you maintain an organized home. With a bit of dedication and effort, you can create a clutter-free home that is easy to maintain.

5A: Regular Cleaning

Regular cleaning is an important part of maintaining a well-organized home. It helps to keep the home free from dust, dirt, and debris, and also helps to keep the home looking and feeling tidy. There are several steps that should be taken on a regular basis to ensure that the home is kept clean and organized.

The first step in regular cleaning is to dust and vacuum the home. This should be done weekly, or more often if the home is particularly dusty. This will help to keep dust from accumulating and spreading throughout the home. Vacuuming should be done on a regular basis, as it helps to remove dirt and debris from carpets and other surfaces.

The next step in regular cleaning is to mop and sweep the home. This should be done every other week, or more often if needed. Mopping and sweeping helps to keep the floors clean and free from dirt and debris. It is important to use a quality cleaner for this step, as it will help to ensure that the floor is properly cleaned.

The third step in regular cleaning is to wipe down surfaces. This should be done weekly, or more often if the surfaces are particularly dirty. Wiping down surfaces helps to keep the home looking neat and tidy, as well as helps to prevent the spread of dirt and bacteria.

The fourth step in regular cleaning is to clean windows and mirrors. This should be done every other week, or more often if needed. Cleaning windows and mirrors helps to keep them looking their best, as well as helps to reduce the amount of dust and dirt on them.

Finally, the fifth step in regular cleaning is to clean the bathroom. This should be done on a weekly basis, or more often if the bathroom is particularly dirty. Cleaning the bathroom helps to keep it looking and feeling fresh and clean, as well as helps to reduce the amount of germs and bacteria in the bathroom.

By following these five steps on a regular basis, homeowners can ensure that their home is kept clean and organized. Regular cleaning is the key to maintaining a well-organized home, and can help to improve the overall look and feel of the home.

5B: Staying on Track

Organizational success is a long-term journey, and staying on track is a key factor in reaching the desired outcome. Whether the goal is to declutter your home, office, or wardrobe, it's important to have strategies in place to stay motivated and prevent backsliding.

Establishing a routine is one of the most effective ways to maintain a successful decluttering program. Setting aside a specific time each day to focus on organizing and tidying will help to keep the project on track. It is also important to set realistic expectations. It is impossible to declutter an entire home in one day, so break the project down into manageable chunks and set achievable goals.

Another important factor in staying on track is to prioritize. Start with the areas that have the most clutter and then move on to the smaller tasks. It can be helpful to keep a list of tasks that need to be completed and mark them off as they are accomplished. This will help keep the momentum going and keep the project from becoming overwhelming.

It's also important to reward yourself for the progress you make. Celebrate the small victories and reward yourself for completing tasks. This will help to keep you motivated and make the process more enjoyable.

Finally, it's important to stay organized. Create a system that works for you and make sure you stick to it. This may involve separating items into different categories or organizing them in a specific way. Find a system that works for you and make sure to keep it up.

Staying on track while organizing your home can be a challenge, but it is possible with the right strategies. Establish a routine, set realistic expectations, prioritize, reward yourself, and stay organized. With these tips, you will be on your way to a more organized and decluttered home.

Chapter 6: Finishing Up

By the time you reach the end of this book, you should have a clearer understanding of what it takes to declutter your home and create a more organized life. You may have already made a lot of progress and are feeling proud of your accomplishments. However, it is important to remember that decluttering is an ongoing process and it is important to stay on top of it.

Organizing your belongings can be a daunting task, but it does not have to be overwhelming. Start by taking small steps and working your way up. Break down each task into manageable chunks and focus on one task at a time. This will make the process more manageable and help you stay motivated.

Above all, make sure to make decluttering your home a priority. Even if it is just a few minutes a day, dedicating a bit of time to getting organized can make a big difference. You may even find that it helps you feel more productive and organized in other aspects of your life.

When you are feeling overwhelmed or discouraged, take a break and come back to it later. Decluttering can be a long process, and it is important to stay motivated. Consider enlisting the help of a friend or family member if you need extra support.

Before you know it, your home will be organized and decluttered. Once you have achieved this goal, it is important to remember to keep your home organized. Set aside time each week to tidy up and put away any items that you have been using. This will help you keep your home clean and organized.

Organizing your home can be a rewarding and satisfying experience. With the right attitude and a little bit of persistence, you can create an organized and decluttered home. Take it one step at a time and remember that it is worth it in the end.

6A: Celebrating Success

Success in home organization is a great accomplishment. It can be a long journey of changes, but it can also be incredibly rewarding. To celebrate the success of reaching a home organization goal, it is important to recognize the small victories that have been achieved and to give yourself the recognition you deserve.

First, take a moment to appreciate the hard work and dedication that went into reaching the goal. This could be acknowledging the effort and time that went into implementing a new system, or simply taking note of the progress that has been made since the journey began.

To celebrate the success, it is important to recognize the progress that has been made and to reward yourself. This reward can be a simple as patting yourself on the back, or it could be something a bit more special. It could be a night out with friends, a spa day, or a special treat. Whatever it is, make sure to make time for yourself and to reward yourself for the progress that has been made.

It is also important to take note of the success and to document it. This could be as simple as writing a journal entry, or it could be recording a video. By documenting the success it is possible to look back and to reflect on the journey and the progress that has been made.

Finally, it is important to share the success with others. Share it with friends and family, or even with the wider world if you feel comfortable doing so. Sharing the success can help to motivate and inspire others, and it can also be a great way to look back on the journey and the progress that has been made.

By celebrating the success that has been achieved in home organization, it is possible to recognize the effort and dedication that went into reaching the goal. It is important to reward yourself for the progress that has been made, to take note of the success and to document it, and to share it with others if it feels right to do so. Doing so can make the journey even more rewarding and can help to motivate and inspire others.

6B: Preparing for the Future

As the saying goes, "Failing to plan is planning to fail." Home organization is no exception. Although it is easy to become overwhelmed by the task of sorting, decluttering, and organizing one's home, it is important to remember to plan for the future. Doing so will make the process much smoother and help to maintain a clean and organized living space.

The first step in preparing for the future is to create a plan. Consider the goals you want to achieve with your home organization project. Are you looking to create more storage space? Are you wanting to make the house more aesthetically pleasing? Are you looking to streamline your daily routine? Whatever your goals may be, write them down and create a plan to accomplish them.

The second step is to create a timeline. It is important to set realistic expectations for yourself and create a timeline to help you stay on track. Break down the project into smaller tasks and prioritize them. Be sure to give yourself enough time to complete each task without becoming overwhelmed.

The third step is to create a budget. Estimate the cost of any materials or services you may need to complete your project. This includes any organizing containers, storage, furniture, or professional organizing services. As with the timeline, it is important to be realistic with your budget and only purchase what you need.

The fourth step is to declutter. This is often the most daunting part of the home organization process, but it is also the most important. Create a pile for items you want to keep, donate, or throw away. Go through each room carefully and be honest with yourself about what you need and what you don't.

The fifth step is to organize. Once you have decluttered, it is time to start organizing. Use containers, shelves, and drawers to create a system that works for you. Be sure to label everything and make sure everything has its own place.

Finally, it is important to maintain the organization. Keep up with your daily routine and take the time to put things back in their place. Once a week, take the time to do a deep clean and reorganize any items that have been displaced.

Preparing for the future is an important part of the home organization process. By creating a plan, timeline, budget, and maintaining an organized home, you will be able to enjoy a clean and clutter-free living space for years to come.

Printed in Great Britain
by Amazon

23367489R00030